Pebb

The Calendar

Months

by Patricia J. Murphy

Consulting Editor: Gail Saunders-Smith, PhD

Capstone press
Mankato, Minnesota

Pebble Books are published by Capstone Press,
1710 Roe Crest Drive, North Mankato, Minnesota 56003.
www.capstonepub.com

Library of Congress Cataloging-in-Publication Data
Murphy, Patricia J., 1963–
Months / by Patricia J. Murphy.
p. cm.—(The calendar)
Includes bibliographical references and index.
13-digit: 978-0-7368-3628-9 (library binding)
10-digit: 0-7368-3628-4 (library binding)
13-digit: 978-0-7368-5075-9 (softcover pbk.)
10-digit: 0-7368-5075-9 (softcover pbk.)
1. Calendar—Juvenile literature. 2. Months—Juvenile literature. I. Title.
CE13.M874 2005
529'.2—dc22

2004011902

Note to Parents and Teachers

The Calendar set supports national social studies and history standards related to time, place, and change. This book describes and illustrates months. The images support early readers in understanding the text. The repetition of words and phrases helps early readers learn new words. This book also introduces early readers to subject-specific vocabulary words, which are defined in the Glossary section. Early readers may need assistance to read some words and to use the Table of Contents, Glossary, Read More, Internet Sites, and Index sections of the book.

Printed in the United States of America in North Mankato, Minnesota.
032012
006646R

Table of Contents

What Is a Month?

A month is one of the 12 parts of a year. Each month lasts 28 to 31 days.

How many days are in each month?

Thirty days have September,
April, June, and November.
All the rest have 31,
Excepting February alone,
Which has 28 days clear,
But 29 each leap year.

The Calendar

January

Sunday	Monday	Tuesday	Wednesday	Thursday	Friday	Saturday
		1	2	3	4	5
6	7	8	9	10	11	12
13	14	15	16	17	18	19
20	21	22	23	24	25	26
27	28	29	30	31		

February

Sunday	Monday	Tuesday	Wednesday	Thursday	Friday	Saturday
					1	2
3	4	5	6	7	8	9
10	11	12	13	14	15	16
17	18	19	20	21	22	23
24	25	26	27	28		

March

Sunday	Monday	Tuesday	Wednesday	Thursday	Friday	Saturday
					1	2
3	4	5	6	7	8	9
10	11	12	13	14	15	16
17	18	19	20	21	22	23
24/31	25	26	27	28	29	30

April

Sunday	Monday	Tuesday	Wednesday	Thursday	Friday	Saturday
	1	2	3	4	5	6
7	8	9	10	11	12	13
14	15	16	17	18	19	20
21	22	23	24	25	26	27
28	29	30				

May

Sunday	Monday	Tuesday	Wednesday	Thursday	Friday	Saturday
			1	2	3	4
5	6	7	8	9	10	11
12	13	14	15	16	17	18
19	20	21	22	23	24	25
26	27	28	29	30	31	

June

Sunday	Monday	Tuesday	Wednesday	Thursday	Friday	Saturday
						1
2	3	4	5	6	7	8
9	10	11	12	13	14	15
16	17	18	19	20	21	22
23/30	24	25	26	27	28	29

July

Sunday	Monday	Tuesday	Wednesday	Thursday	Friday	Saturday
	1	2	3	4	5	6
7	8	9	10	11	12	13
14	15	16	17	18	19	20
21	22	23	24	25	26	27
28	29	30	31			

August

Sunday	Monday	Tuesday	Wednesday	Thursday	Friday	Saturday
				1	2	3
4	5	6	7	8	9	10
11	12	13	14	15	16	17
18	19	20	21	22	23	24
25	26	27	28	29	30	31

September

Sunday	Monday	Tuesday	Wednesday	Thursday	Friday	Saturday
1	2	3	4	5	6	7
8	9	10	11	12	13	14
15	16	17	18	19	20	21
22	23	24	25	26	27	28
29	30					

October

Sunday	Monday	Tuesday	Wednesday	Thursday	Friday	Saturday
		1	2	3	4	5
6	7	8	9	10	11	12
13	14	15	16	17	18	19
20	21	22	23	24	25	26
27	28	29	30	31		

November

Sunday	Monday	Tuesday	Wednesday	Thursday	Friday	Saturday
					1	2
3	4	5	6	7	8	9
10	11	12	13	14	15	16
17	18	19	20	21	22	23
24	25	26	27	28	29	30

December

Sunday	Monday	Tuesday	Wednesday	Thursday	Friday	Saturday
1	2	3	4	5	6	7
8	9	10	11	12	13	14
15	16	17	18	19	20	21
22	23	24	25	26	27	28
29	30	31				

The calendar shows that one month is about four weeks long.

First Months of the Year

January and February
are the first months
of the year.
Laura wears warm clothes
during these cold months.

The weather warms up in March. Laura plants seeds with her dad.

April can be
a rainy month.
Laura needs an umbrella.
The rain helps flowers
grow in May.

Middle of the Year

The school year ends in June. Laura starts summer vacation. She goes to camp in July.

In August, Laura shops for new school clothes. She starts school again in September.

Last Months of the Year

In October, Laura dresses up for Halloween. In November, she eats Thanksgiving dinner.

In December, Laura wraps gifts for her family. December is the last month of the year.

Glossary

calendar—a chart that shows all of the days, weeks, and months in a year; some calendars show one day, one week, or one month at a time.

day—a period of time that equals 24 hours; each month has between 28 and 31 days.

leap year—a year that has 366 days caused by an extra day in February; a leap year comes every four years.

week—a period of seven days from Sunday to Saturday; there are about four weeks in a month.

year—a period of 12 months; the year begins on January 1 and ends on December 31.

Read More

Brode, Robyn. *January.* Months of the Year. Milwaukee: Weekly Reader Early Learning Library, 2003.

Kummer, Patricia K. *The Calendar.* Inventions that Shaped the World. New York: Franklin Watts, 2005.

Nelson, Robin. *Months.* First Step Nonfiction. Minneapolis: Lerner, 2002.

Internet Sites

FactHound offers a safe, fun way to find Internet sites related to this book. All of the sites on FactHound have been researched by our staff.

Here's how:

1. Visit *www.facthound.com*
2. Type in this special code **0736836284** for age-appropriate sites. Or enter a search word related to this book for a more general search.
3. Click on the **Fetch It** button.

FactHound will fetch the best sites for you!

Index

Word Count: 135
Grade: 1
Early-Intervention Level: 10

Editorial Credits
Sarah L. Schuette, editor; Jennifer Bergstrom, set designer

Photo Credits
All photographs by James Photography/James Menk